100+ Dirty Jokes

LOL Funny Jokes Club

Copyright © 2016 LOL Funny Jokes Club

All rights reserved.

ISBN-13: 978-1535541541
ISBN-10: 1535541547

DEDICATION

This book is dedicated everyone in the world that enjoys a good laugh. Laughter is one of the best gifts you can give.

CONTENTS

DEDICATION iii

DIRTY JOKES 1

ABOUT THE AUTHOR 29

DIRTY JOKES

Q: Why are condoms like cameras?

A: They both capture the moment.

Q: What did the sign on the whore house say?

A: Beat it we are closed!

Q: You know the worst thing about oral sex?

A: The view.

Q: Why do men become smarter during sex?

A: Because they are plugged into a genius.

Q: Why is sex like a game of bridge?

A: You don't need a partner if you have a good hand.

Q: Is it sexual harassment if you go to a woman and tell her that her hair smells nice?

A: What if the man is a dwarf?

Q: What's one thing everybody sees in a blonde?

A: A dick.

Q: What's the difference between Indiana and a blonde?

A: A blonde has larger hills and deeper valleys.

Q: What is the definition of the perfect woman?

A: A deaf and dumb, blonde nymphomaniac whose father owns a pub.

Q: What does a screen door and a blonde have in common?

A: The more you bang it the looser it gets.

Q: How can you tell who a blonde's boyfriend is?

A: He's the one with the belt buckle that matches the impression in her forehead.

Q: How can you tell when a blonde is dating?

A: By the buckle print on her forehead.

Q: How does a blonde interpret 6.9?

A: A 69 interrupted by a period.

Q: Why does NASA hire peroxide blondes?

A: They're doing research on black holes.

Q: What do you call two blondes in a canoe?

A: Fur traders.

Q: What is 68 to a blonde?

A: Where she goes down on you and you owe her one.

Q: Why do blondes get confused in the ladies room?

A: They have to pull their own pants down.

Q: Why is a blonde like Australia?

A: They're both down under, and no one cares.

Q: What did the blonde say during a porno?

A: There I am!

Q: What's the difference between sin and shame?

A: It is a sin to put it in, but it's a shame to pull it out.

Q: What does a blonde say after multiple orgasms?

A: Way to go team.

Q: What's the difference between a blonde and McDonalds?

A: A blonde serves more people in a night.

Q: What's the difference between a blonde and an ironing board?

A: It's difficult to open the legs of an ironing board.

Q: What does a blonde answer to the question, "Are you sexually active?"

A: No, I just lie there.

Q: What do you call a blonde with a bag of sugar on her head?

A: Sweet fuck all.

Q: What did the blondes left leg say to her right leg?

A: Between the two of us, we can make a lot of money.

Q: What is a bellybutton for?

A: It gives a blonde a place to park her gum on the way down.

Q: Why did the blonde give a blow job after sex?

A: She wanted to have her cock and eat it too.

Q: What is the smartest thing that can come out of a blonde's mouth?

A: Einstein's dick.

Q: What do you call a blonde that can suck a golfball through a water hose?

A: Sweetheart!

Q: What did the blind blonde say as she was making love with her new boyfriend?

A: Funny, you don't feel Jewish.

Q: What do blondes have against condoms?

A: Their cheeks.

Q: Why did the blonde guy put ice in his condom?

A: To keep the swelling down.

Q: Why did the blonde guy ask his girlfriend to squeeze his left testicle?

A: Because the road sign said squeeze left.

Q: Why did the blonde have a hysterectomy?

A: She wanted to stop having grandchildren.

Q: Why did the blonde make love in the microwave?

A: She wanted to have a baby in 9 minutes.

Q: What do you call 1,000 heavily armed lesbians?

A: Militia Etheridge.

Q: What did the leper say to the hooker?

A: Keep the tip.

Q: Why does a blonde insist on him wearing a condom?

A: So she can have a doggie bag for later.

Q: Why do blondes always drink with straws?

A: Practice.

Q: My husband and I divorced over religious differences.

A: He thought he was God, and I didn't.

Q: Why does a bride smile when she walks up the aisle?

A: She knows she's given her last blow job.

Q: How is a woman like a condom?

A: Both of them spend more time in your wallet than on your dick.

Q: What is the definition of making love?

A: Something a woman does while a guy is f*cking her.

Q: Did you ever blow bubbles as child?

A: Yeah, well he's back in town and wants your new number.

Q: Why do blondes have orgasms?

A: So they know when to stop having sex.

Q: How can you tell if a blonde works in an office?

A: A bed in the stockroom and huge smiles on all the bosses faces.

Q: What do you call 4 blondes lying on the beach?

A: Public access.

Q: How does a horny guy spell relief?

A: B-L-O-N-D-E.

Q: How does a blonde prepare for safe sex?

A: She puts on rubber based lipstick.

Q: Why did the blonde give up bowling for screwing?

A: The balls are lighter and you don't have to change shoes.

Q: Did you hear about the conceited blonde?

A: She screams her own name when she comes.

Q: What do you call a brunette and three blondes in a corner?

A: You don't, you see if you've got 3 condoms.

Q: How can you tell who the head nurse of a facility is?

A: She's the one with dirty knees.

Q: Did you know that a condom has a serial number?

A: No, I never had to unroll one that far.

Q: What is hard, six inches long, has two nuts, and can make a girl fat?

A: Almond Joy candy bars!

Q: What is a four-letter word that ends in k and means the same as intercourse?

A: Talk.

Q: Did you hear the slogan for the new Stealth Condom?

A: They'll never see you coming.

Q: What's the definition of a teenager?

A: God's punishment for enjoying sex.

Q: What do you call kinky sex with chocolate?

A: S&M&M.

Q: What do you call a truckload of vibrators?

A: Toys for Twats.

Q: What's the definition of a Yankee?

A: Same thing as a quickie, only you do it yourself.

Q: What has seventy-five balls and screws old ladies?

A: Bingo!

Q: How are men are like cement?

A: After getting laid, they take a long time to get hard.

Q: How are women and rocks alike?

A: You skip across the flat ones.

Q: What is it when a man talks dirty to a woman?

A: Sexual harassment.

Q: What comes after 69?

A: Mouthwash.

Q: What do men and sperm have in common?

A: They both have a one-in-a-million chance of becoming a human being.

Q: What does a woman's asshole do when she is having an orgasm?

A: He is usually home with the kids!

Q: What did the egg say to the boiling water?

A: How can you expect me to get hard so fast? I just got laid a minute ago.

Q: What is the difference between a frog and a horny toad?

A: One says ribbit ribbit, the other one says rub-it, rub-it!

Q: Why did the condom cross the road?

A: Because it was pissed off.

Q: Why do men masturbate?

A: It is sex with someone they love.

Q: What did the elephant say to the naked man?

A: It's cute but can you pick up peanuts with it?

Q: Why are cowgirls bowlegged?

A: Cowboys like to eat with their hats on.

Q: What did the Indian say to the white woman when she tied his penis in a knot?

A: How come?

Q: How many perverts does it take to put in a light bulb?

A: Just one, but it takes the entire emergency room to get it out!

Q: What did the cannibal do after he dumped his girlfriend?

A: Wiped his ass.

Q: How do you embarrass an archeologist?

A: Give him a used tampon and ask him which period it came from.

Q: What's the difference between a g-spot and a golf ball?

A: A guy will actually search for a golf ball.

Q: What's the difference between getting a divorce and getting circumcised?

A: When you get a divorce, you get rid of the whole prick!

Q: What's the difference between a Catholic wife and a Jewish wife?

A: A Catholic wife has real orgasms and fake jewelry.

Q: What do you call a lesbian dinosaur?

A: A Lickalotopus.

Q: Which sexual position produces the ugliest children?

A: Ask your mother.

Q: What do you call a gay dinosaur?

A: Mega-sore-ass.

Q: Why did Frosty the Snowman pull down his pants?

A: He heard the snow blower coming.

Q: What can a goose do, a duck can't, and a lawyer should?

A: Stick his bill up his ass.

Q: Why is food better than men?

A: Because you don't have to wait an hour for seconds.

Q: What have men and spray paint in common?

A: One squeeze and they're all over you.

Q: What do elephants use for tampons?

A: Sheep.

Q: What's the difference between a mosquito and a blonde?

A: When you slap a mosquito, it will stop sucking.

Q: What's another name for pickled bread?

A: Dill-dough.

Q: How do you annoy your girlfriend during sex?

A: Phone her.

Q: Why do hunters make the best lovers?

A: Because they go deep in the bush, shoot more than once and they eat what they shoot.

Q: What's the difference between premenstrual tension and BSE?

A: One's mad cow disease, the others an agricultural problem.

Q: Why is the space between a woman's breasts and her hips called a waist?

A: Because you could easily fit another pair of tits in there.

Q: What's the definition of love, true love, and showing off?

A: Spitting, swallowing and gargling.

Q: What's the difference between your wife and your job?

A: After 10 years, the job still sucks.

Q: If the dove is the bird of peace, what is the bird of true love?

A: The swallow.

Q: Why did God create women?

A: To carry semen from the bedroom to the toilet.

Q: Why is Viagra like Disneyworld?

A: You have to wait an hour for a three minute ride.

Q: What's the difference between oral sex and anal sex?

A: Oral sex makes your day, anal sex makes your hole weak.

Q: What should you do if your girlfriend starts smoking?

A: Slow down and use a lubricant.

Q: Why do divorced men get married again?

A: Bad memory.

Q: Why is divorce so expensive?

A: Because it's worth it.

ABOUT THE AUTHOR

The LOL Funny Jokes Club is dedicated to comedy. We'll tickle your funny bone with our side-splitting jokes and humor. Whether it's funny and hilarious one-liners, hilarious jokes, or laugh-out-loud rib tickling knee slappers, the LOL Funny Jokes Club does it all!

For more funny joke books just search for
LOL FUNNY JOKES CLUB on Amazon

Printed in Great Britain
by Amazon